More Naked Than Ever

More Naked Than Ever

GW Rasberry

First Edition

Hidden Brook Press
www.HiddenBrookPress.com
writers@HiddenBrookPress.com

Copyright © 2013 Hidden Brook Press
Copyright © 2013 Gary Rasberry

All rights for poems revert to the author. All rights for book, layout and design remain with Hidden Brook Press. No part of this book may be reproduced except by a reviewer who may quote brief passages in a review. The use of any part of this publication reproduced, transmitted in any form or by any means, electronic, mechanical, photocopied, recorded or otherwise stored in a retrieval system without prior written consent of the publisher is an infringement of the copyright law.

More Naked Than Ever
by GW Rasberry

Editor – Bruce Kauffman
Front Cover Photograph – Catherine Nocera
Cover Design – Richard M. Grove
Layout and Design – Richard M. Grove

Typeset in Garamond
Printed and bound in USA

Library and Archives Canada Cataloguing in Publication

Rasberry, Gary William, 1959-, author
    More naked than ever / GW Rasberry.

Poems.
ISBN 978-1-927725-04-7 (pbk.)

    I. Title.

PS8635.A72M67 2013   C811'.6   C2013-905936-9

If I loose my grip will I take flight?

—*Bruce Cockburn*

Contents

Through a Poet's I – *p. 1*
Worth Staying Up Late For – *p. 2*
For the View – *p. 3*
Writing Songs – *p. 4*
Prose into Poetry – *p. 5*

Wisdom Come – *p. 6*
Writing About Writing – *p. 7*
A Tiny Note – *p. 8*
The Rush – *p. 9*
Skin of My Teeth – *p. 10*
The Steps We Took to Get Here – *p. 13*

Commuter Portfolio – *p. 15*
How Miserable – *p. 17*
The Eagles en Français – *p. 19*
All Lonely People – *p. 22*
Hospital Waiting Room – *p. 24*
Without a Manual – *p. 25*

Sways Heavy – *p. 26*
Stunt Girl – *p. 28*
More Naked Than Ever – *p. 30*
Lovers – *p. 33*
Erotic Fiction – *p. 36*

Half-Full for Sure – *p. 47*
A Font for All Occasions – *p. 49*
Resilience – *p. 51*
No One but the Moon – *p. 53*
Field Notes for Jabez – *p. 54*
Great Big Love – *p. 57*
Another Poem for You – *p. 59*

End Notes – *p. 63*
Author Bio Note – *p. 65*

Through a Poet's I

Eye seem to have a poet's I.
Not for any particular rhyme or

reason. Maybe it's just because
I have always been

will always be
unfinished.

Uncomfortable in happiness.
Incomplete in unhappiness.

Confident in introspection.
One I down the road.

One eye out for beauty:
Always and Ever.

Worth Staying Up Late For

How late does one have to stay up
to write a song? Make love
rhyme with orange?
Place sadness on the window sill
where the moon might replace it

with a note for the morning sun
to remember nothing of what was said
in anger the night before.

How naked? How beautiful?
Longing and longing.
It's nothing like they said

it would be. Holding hands
with nothing but the night wind
strumming the dark pines and

stars scattered in the back yard.
Music dreams everyone
toward a surprise of lost memory.

We take our places for the opening
curtain with quiet purpose: a falling
down fence welcomes the late stragglers.

Poems are handed out
under street lamps warm and yellowy.
Pools of light remind us of those

who aren't quite here
yet. And we all know who
we are just this once.

For the View
—*for RBU*

Climbing up out of words
for the view and all
that it affords.

Downstream the sounds surround
you and leave you
without worry.

How far ahead do we need
to see? How clear the picture?
If we measure every day and spend

the rest our lives doing
the math? Vision for vision's
sake. The sun tries harder

each day to remind us to keep faith
held loosely. Light growing
in the tiniest of increments.

And love, too. Love that we know
we deserve but still keep two fingers
crossed behind our back and ask kindly
after humility. Offer sweet
condolence to those who still wait.

Count blessings and offer ourselves
up without fear. For love and
for the view.

Writing Songs

You write it down or else it's gone
You write it down you build a song

Not to worry about the time
signature but a beat missing can make
all the difference. To close your eyes

and see the lines fall out across
fields and lift up into melody.
Hearing is believing.

Listening in for what may not be
there. Words don't seem to mind
being asked to dance. Wallflower'd
poems quite willing to go all the way.

Love always and already available
for reinvention. The heart will
follow the muse with just a whispered
promise. Words quite willing

to bleed for the stones pushed
uphill. Or the narrow path inward
and twisting. Faith and the horizon

and every song ever written. Your
life made different for all the ways
you have been sung.

With all of your might you never
truly believe until you find yourself
writing songs.

Cuz' if you don't you'll never know
That this is how your lifeline flows …

Prose into Poetry

Can prose become
 poetry simply
 by bending
 itself or even breaking
 so that the words fly
 down from their delicate perches
 and fall into new
 configurations?

Can the different ways
we line our world
also give shape to the ways we live
our lives?

One can only
 hope.

Wisdom Come

And when will the days of wisdom come?
And the arrival of Thy Will be done?

Maybe when no words follow.
Just noise and quiet and in between.

The poet's feelings secure beyond hurt
and nothing needing to be fixed.

Clear and cryptic.

Out the window just a glimpse
of the next door neighbour's roofline:
glorious snowy peak. Steep pitch
and full of story. For an instant: the Himalayas.
For an instant: the next door neighbour's roofline.
For an instant: one and the same.

And when further exploration
leads to nothing in particular and a
deepened line of inquiry makes no more
sense, noise and quiet follow.
The poet and nothing
in between.
.
Stick figures roped together climb
steadily. The snowline brilliant.
For an instant the summit made
possible by the laborious laying
down of word after word.

The mountain. The window.
The next door neighbours.
The glimpse of story: one
and the same.

Writing About Writing

Question: Why write
about writing
when you could be
writing?

Answers: Please choose any
or all of the following:

Caffeine. Writing is covered by
OHIP. Your doctoral committee
insists. Self-reflexivity
is your first   language.

Post-structuralism was having a fire
sale your first year of grad school.

Caffeine.

Best ask Natalie Goldberg.
Writing about writing is an unavoidable
pain pleasure pain pleasure pain

pleasure. Why not? Why a navel if not
for gazing? Caffeine. Psychotherapy
is not covered by OHIP. Who is
Natalie Goldberg?

A Tiny Note

The man of letters runs out of words
The waves grow steep—there are clouds and birds
He can love her and she can love him
Though they've both run out of words.

The ocean sings a thousand names
The moon forgives the sun its games
She can love him and he can love her
Though they've both forgotten their names.

So lost in the middle one does forget
The shape of the shoreline the weight of the debt
We can love love and love can love us
It just hasn't happened yet.

You shed your sweater you shed your coat
You write yourself a tiny note:
If we can't love ourselves there is no hope
And we're all in the self-same boat.

The forest girl takes off her clothes
Arrives at the place where no one knows
We want to love but we don't know how
This part of the story goes.

He looked for love in the middle of living
And gave himself for the sake of giving
So this is love and now we know
The frozen stars there shimmering.

We soon let go because there's no sense holding
The weight of Every Thing unfolding
So this is Love and how we know
Beholden and beholding.

The Rush
—for Alan Travers

Of movement. Colours
twisted into patterns
crude and lovely.
A sweaty elegance, really.

What would you have seen? Heard?

I can't say for the pounding
of pictures inside my own head.
Or maybe it was my Ego stuffed larger
than the image of the instant metal
kissed ice.

It's all so big and wild and full
and intense that I forget
what it feels like, try hard
to sharpen words into a point
of view that might provide anything
but a blur of bodies

Working at play
bordering on religion—
a crazed misfortune of genetics
that has brought boys to the height
of manhood only

To curl in on itself in cruel
reversal: How could something light
enough to float weigh so heavy in the hands
of some so bent in heavenly pursuit
that violence provides the only lever
to crack frozen moments in two.

And others to still time
with ancient carvings of
wood and ice so brilliant that
the risk is everything worth
fighting for.

Skin of My Teeth

By the skin of my teeth the days go without mention of death, fire, flood, famine, terror. Just the days. Going by. Quiet. Noisy prayer. Search and Rescue. Purposeful Study. Slushy streets. A wave of an encounter. Suspension. Fear of commitment. More prayer. Pedal steel soundtrack. December meets January meets February. Thoughts of escape. Without mention of fear, anxiety, dread. Life without coffee. Standing on a bridge under repair. There's a party going on somewhere. Children wait to be heard. One father hears rumours of transcendence. Life has come down to this. January with a limp. String quartet suggests something warmer, greener, closer to the sun.

It comes down to this: the breath. An invitation to be present. *One moment, please: your call is important to us.* Important to me. A steady job. Money. Love. Self-respect. Journal entries that may or may not see the light of day. Black tea with milk and honey. Winter sidewalk cafés. There will always be these people. The newspaper, warm boots. Acoustic comforts. Strangers. Despair. Stone walls, red brick facades. Overcast. Main street: the movie. Close-out sales. Love unaccompanied. Love and the silver coin half-seen through the slush. Cloudy with a chance for last call. All those angels. Seen and unseen.

By the skin of my teeth the nights are without light. Not dark, but darker. Not silent night but haunted quiet. Breathe held. Blankets pulled up. Cold pressing against the windows. Midnight sweats. Black. Heavy blackness, not like the sky without stars but like space. Deep. Unknown. Ice and snow.

I'm here. Half-way up the hill in the darker darkness. Not to be thought about. Fear is the curtain pulled tight-shut. Not so easy to make friends with the dark. If someone is playing the piano downstairs, they're playing quietly. Or noisily without sound. Just a mad hammering of thoughts, the melody flying half-mast and shredded.

Where does courage come from? Knowing just beyond the edge of thought that the day will force itself up, like a cardboard prop handled by amateur stage-hands. The Sun has been given a pink slip. Laid off but unable not to work. A pale distant burning. Cold comfort.

I am not writing this. The woodstove never lights itself. Ashes to ashes. Dropping down and falling backward to forgive. Some Mystery that you sort of want to solve. Write toward longer light. Forgiveness for All and for All a Good Night. Write longer toward light. I am writing this.

By the skin so we go. Cloud-thin, sleepy blue, tired gray, cloud-thin. There he goes thinking by. Like walking without the calorie loss. Thin-skinned. Thinking of all the better ways.

Lovely tired. Sink and float. Glass skin. Stone walls stacked high. Always concrete and an opportunity to use 'ubiquitous.' Middle distance time travels. Stained glass. Reputations. Won. Lost. More cars. Slow motion makes them seem safer. Wheeled rhythms. More walking. Ambulatory meditations. Idle chatter. Self-importance. Regardless. Red brick, too. Singer-songwriters need not apply. Morning erotics. Hustle bustle. So much the weather can not help us say. Major and minor. Where do they all go? Where do we? Do I?

By the skin of my teeth, for certain. Poems re-writing themselves. A decade later. Taking things in stride. An easy backbeat. Fur collars. A beautiful scarf. Acoustic enough. The sky flat. Generosity footnoted. Wool mittens. Never so complete. Take the melody and know that we know. Take one step back. Two more. Soften the skin. Down to breath. The cello will make a brief appearance shortly. Loosely in tune. Down the road. Like walking. By our skin we go.

Skin, by and by. Snow today. Another beautiful mess. Friends are everywhere. Thanking God now. Standing on coffee's threshold, walking the plank with calm certainty. A pill between me and my anxiety'd morning. Everything Serious. Now. Always. Don't lose your nerve. Is it too late to become a recognized and respected figure on the street? Being caring and neurotic and kind lacks a certain sex appeal. Slush on the street dreams me warmer. It doesn't even have to be a rain forest. White. Middle. Class. Angst. And yet. And yet. *The door that closes tightly is the door that can swing wide.* (I didn't write this. Daniel Lanois sang it.) Just to keep writing, head up, head down, just to keep writing. And what about those scraggly butt-ugly leaves that don't ever fall from January's tree. Ugliness is in the eye of the beholder, traffic waxing, waning. Another beautiful friend. Snow on skin, my daughter's tongue, too. A plank to walk to God. Anxiety's threshold. Morning and me. Now. Always.

The Steps We Took to Get Here
—*for H and Z*

All I need to give you two is time.
So easy to keep and give
away   maybe find somewhere
else. You two are everything

necessary in the equational
homework we are so often preoccupied
with. No need even to show our
work in the margin. Don't have to
show the steps we took to get here.

We *know* how we got the answer
and that's that. Look it up
in the back   of the book
if you like. Be our guest but we know

(not for sure mind you) but we
pretty much know that we have it
made. That's how much love

can't be solved for 'x.' The variables:
there's never a question of 'if'
or 'whether.' There are. There will be.
There must be   many.

Variables.

Confounding and otherwise
my only job is to be there
in the back of the book or here
just quietly minding the store.
But who works the cash?

You two do. That's who. And that's
just fine. It really is because being there
is my job. That's what pays. Being
there. And here, too. Here I am
also being there. There and here.
All at once. Happily.
With you two. All I need.
Bless and keep you and
everything you are and
ever will be.   Only time

will tell. Meantime we just
know. And that's all
we will ever need.

Commuter Portfolio
Utrecht to The Haag: Amsterdam, The Netherlands

I am surrounded now
by the young who run
on the strength of the beauty of not
knowing they are young. They do not need to
know anything more
for now. It's best this way.
Best not to know.

Delicate moss greens the rooftops
from the train moving
away and toward. The landscape
moves to keep me
still.

In Central Station, the flow
of bodies changes nothing.
Vanity and loss are mine
to let go and embrace.

Asking for directions, I come close
to disappearing. I apply and
reapply for visas. For admittance, for
entry into my own
skin. Some conditions may
and will apply. Strictly
speaking.

Language humbles
me.   So much
to not understand. On the

platform, more girls
light cigarettes. The smoke becomes
them. The privacy of the public
space always ruptured by the ubiquitous
mobile phone: one-way
conversations much louder
than one would ever want or need.
Italian amplified through a Dutch accent.

Who would ever be so hopeful and
foolish to put their finger in
the dike? Still, the windmill holds
iconic stature for the way it so easily
invites the wind to pass through without
contract or talk of harnessing
anything. Energy cannot be
created nor destroyed. Try telling that
to the man outside the station wearing three
coats and no shoes. I am surrounded
now by the young and the old who
run on the strength of beauty and its
absence. Becoming
invisible.
I am.

How Miserable

Hey, wanna find out how
miserable you are? Take
a vacation. Take an ocean

cruise where you can't hide
your unhappiness but you can
eat all you want. All the time.

Yes. You can eat non-stop—all
eating all the time. Why bother
digesting when you can go bowling

on deck 6, gamble on deck 7, drink or
shop or maybe just eat some
more. Fill up your empty

day with busy play. Hustle to get to the front
of the omelet line. Dare yourself
to stare hard at the horizon

for longer than your busy mind can tolerate.
(Is it actually a line where all the different blues
come together?) How is this much water

possible? Imagine the cruise
director's jobs on all those war ships carrying young
men to meet death. How miserable you are.

Imagine the first groups of immigrants
who sailed from the Old Country to escape
misery only to find it again in the new.

And all those sailors having a whale
of a time. Imagine the slaughter. And
the history of exploration: kill and move
on. Move on and kill. Columbus all jacked up

on scurvy or syphilis discovering places
he never found. The insanity of the equator
tripping anything or anyone
crazy enough to cross the line.
Hot enough to boil the ocean.
Burn stories into history

textbooks. Or stories
of ice-breakers seeking

fame and open passage. Frozen solid
and going nowhere fast.
So take an ocean cruise. Dare yourself
to kill time without thinking. Find out how
miserable you really are from stem

to stern. Don't forget:
dessert is always
included.

Drinking Cheap but Good Red Wine in the South of France While Listening to The Eagles' Greatest Hits (Zut Alors)

One of these nights..
One of these crazy old nights ...
 —The Eagles

It could have happened to anyone listening
to the "Eagles Greatest Hits" in the South
of France while drinking   red wine.

You got your demons
you got desires ...

Tangled in vines with culverts rushing
bruised and purple full and wild through every stone
village. In any language it's another tequila
sunrise wasted certainement mais even falling
drunk down January's mountainside

It's easy to see
how the light kisses
the grapes that aren't even close
to being here yet and how impossible the whole
enterprise. The soil stubborn gold
rocky and holding on
to thousand-year-old stories

Of how it might be
done if you pray hard
enough imagine a joyless
toil so calloused that blisters bear
fruit. Old men spit and shit

And swear they saw it
coming—a split
second held in slow
motion. Ancient stone abbeys

Cut into stone hillsides Blood
and stone. The cross to bear
so great. *You got your
demons.* Chacque person different
chacque person la même.

Pass the bottle share the shame.
Blessed is Thy Holy Name.
Slow motion and a split
decision. A falcon slices through
your vision. Times like this it's easy

To remember your patient brother your loving
sister. Your parents drunk the night you first
kissed her. And it was music—the song
building but what did you expect
for 3 euros? *Oh, loneliness will blind*

You in between the dark and the light. The woman
with her hair tied back. Her raven voice
a singsong silhouette. Nothing but sleek
profile. Dress over her head now
lifting and falling naked as language.

You got desires.

Traffic snarls are for Paris
only and how naked she is there.
You wish far away and still you come
close. The bottle catches blue
way up the fretless neck: half way
to full throttle. But who could

sing that fucking high?
Oh, coming right behind
you swear I'm going to find you.

Swimming inside
the full throated
swallow. In any
language. Ce que je veux
dire. This is what I see everytime

in the mirror. *One that really*
screams.

All Lonely People in Cafés

*See the lonely boy out on the weekend trying to make it pay.
Can't relate to joy tries to speak and can't begin to say*
                              —Neil Young

The thrum of coffee.
The press of café conversation

urgent and idle
non-life threatening.

Whim and whisper.
Whining and winded.

Would all lonely persons please
raise their hands? Thank you.

The sun slants through the street facing
windows. Everything is still

possible. More and more though
there is less and less the poet is willing

to admit. The raw hunger felt
by the well fed. The flat line that sees

only curves.   A foot in cold water.
Skin that so badly wants   for touch.

Naked. Bare. Skin aches in fact for caress for
tongue for kiss and tell.

Clothes couldn't come off
fast enough.

Shame on the poet! Shame on
shame? Full of it.

We've always known words
would never be enough but no words

are worse. All lonely people. Please.
Facing the window the poet curves

raw conversations. Tongues well fed.
Anonymity hands itself over

to intimacy. More and more.
Everything is still. Whisper touch.

See the lonely admit
how the tongue is

willing to be tied.
Please   would all people?

Hospital Waiting Room
—for CM

Passing out words—enough
for everyone. Our lives made
visible in this instant.

Who will read us? Affirm our
existence? Cross over
the line. Help us catch

our breath. Realize that every word
matters. Remind us how small
we are—how little

we really know. So we must write
in code. Say Everything that needs
saying while giving nothing

away. Risk it all
with nakedness—the best and only
disguise.

Instant words our guide—a little
cross over. Everything in code.
Nothing matters enough

for how little needs to be said.
Affirm our risk. Disguise enough
for Everyone.

So we must write what we don't
know. Give Everything. Our breath
in this instant—disguise realized.

Without a Manual

The cracks are showing.
My cement smile too much
to bear. Too much weight to hold
the whole thing up

in the air. Where does fear
come from? Who wants to
visit The Why?

Fear. How to live
like there isn't any.

How to read the manual
without a manual.

Without a fucking manual
who would? Less is more or less
more. You might also find it
in the index.

Sways Heavy

Two-lane highway. Rural somewhere. Riding this lonely bus. Fat clouds stapled to the sky turn from green to orange to red: another traffic-light sunset. Fir and pine and spruce silhouettes line the roadside like cardboard cut-outs.

A lone car's headlights come up over the hill, two expectant moons. Darkness decides once and for all to declare night: no touch-backs. Riding this lonely bus. No friends or relations just the driver threatening to roll all night. Threatening to drive this thing right off the end of the island.

The bus slices through darkness swaying heavy as we wind up island. Feeling both ends of 'ageless' trapped in the beam of light that pours from a tiny overhead eye. Words stumble into sentences. Drunk and disorderly they walk thin lines hoping not to get caught.

Riding this bus writing short fiction where everyone gets killed or married in the end. You pencil yourself in beside a woman with midnight thighs who knows the ending. Spend the next few miles passing notes and leaning into dangerous curves (dialogue used sparingly). Who knows?

Maybe this one will end up getting published but damned if the bus doesn't stop in the middle of all this blackness and the only other passenger gets out and walks off into the bush. And now it's just you and her and the driver

riding this bus and you'd swear you knew what you were doing until she picks up the manuscript and starts questioning the plot and pointing out split-fucking infinitives.

You're really a poet you tell her: it's what the characters don't say. The manuscript is shot to hell and just about now you're thinking this whole thing is a big mistake when she slides in close enough to read your mind. *This is poetry not pornography* you say. *They can't just. We can't just ...*

Remind me not to marry a writer, she says, pulling her dress back in place. Already, you're busy rewriting this part: a fingernail of moon scratches a question mark somewhere behind your eyes. The bus driver has a wife and three kids at home but he's willing to keep right on going.

Stunt Girl

Red lips that look like they never disappoint ...

Look like she doesn't care
much, smiles a saxophone
smile, laughs out loud
to hear herself laugh
out loud. And those lips: red.

Unfiltered cigarettes are on
tap, low clouds hanging over
well-rehearsed arguments and maybe
they're making a movie of the whole thing:
hand-held, black and white.

Patrons never need introductions, everybody
is on the rocks and she's a stunt girl
hired for the dangerous part and
here it comes: as hard

as you try you can only imagine
limited scenarios—
parts of you in her
mouth tongue mouth tongue moving, no spare
parts. Tits & Ass. Flesh. Hard. Torque.
Moving. In her. On her.

As hard as you try
you will always wish
for a better part because

according to the script, they take you out back and
beat the shit out of you with a rusted pipe for
thinking these thoughts.

How do they know?

And the dying sun always
strikes the concrete pier like this
and the time of day becomes a
point worth debating over
two more.

Still, no one can come close
to her, try to even hum a bar, pal.
All the other typewriter voices
talking overtime but you'll get over it
once you loosen your tie and remember
your daughter's birthday. Still, you can't help
the way you feel: careful

or you'll end up on your knees singing
piss-stained songs with a drunk accordion player
barking pathetic harmonies and dry-heaving
every other chorus or

worse. Knowing red is a colour now,
like any other colour as the credits bleed slowly
across the screen and don't you hate
the way a story can creep up your thigh?

More Naked Then Ever

What if I were to hold you the way
you said you really wanted to be
held? What then?

Who would turn away
first? When being held is what
is most needed?

And what if I saw you
naked? What if? Who would
turn toward the sound
of our voices? Who?

The newness of it all is beautiful
torture. Pure. Beyond the pale
moon off the back porch.

Your skin, too. New in not
holding back pale.
Who wanted?
I did. So did
you.

Without dress you are you
in the fullness of your
beauty.

Language must once again trip
over itself. Make excuses
for introducing itself so early
in the program. If I could hold

you in your pale dress
make you more
naked than ever. Hold
the thought of you more
closely.

Your skin, too. I admit to wanting
you naked. Beauty itself is on
the program. Dressed up naked.

Making love once again
trip up on itself when sneaking up
would have been the best
and least expected.

To be the one to take off
your dress if that is what
you're wearing. Not for
long. It slips off. Falls
away. Grace goes
starboard.

I wish for all of you
and me. Or maybe the wind

pulls your dress up and over
your head: right off.

Right on. Right
off.

The wind has seen us naked
before and will again blow us
sideways twisting
straight upwards.

I can't see the future
for your face. I can't see your face
for the future. It's one of these
anyway and for all the ways
I can't
see.

Lovers

Never a breath you can afford to waste
When you're lovers in a dangerous time.
                    —Bruce Cockburn

Anger: say this word
over and over again. Continue
to repeat as necessary and Let Go ...

1. Anger (raw)
Angry? Of course you're
fucking angry. Of course
you feel hurt. The heart doesn't

know what the hell it's doing:
it's innocent. Innocent as
hell that's what it is. It wants to be

open. It wants to be
closed. It gets hurt but

it doesn't bleed. Yet the head
is so much worse. So much
worse. (All that thinking.)

It's hard work being evolved
isn't it? Speaking your truth.
Trying to do the right
thing   always.
Yes you must love
yourself   first.

No one wants to get hurt.
No one. You try to love
others the way you want
to be loved yourself.
The truth will set you
free.

2. Anger (cynical)
Oh, maybe it's a
test? Maybe it's all
your fault. Maybe you were supposed
to say, "No, you're wrong!
I *can* be happy. I can work
through all my stuff,
you'll see."

Yes, maybe it *is*
a   test.

3. Anger (sadness)
Sadness sits underneath
anger. Don't we all know
this? And then love
makes its way through
sadness.

Love and sadness: might it be
they are being asked
to do something together?
Something   more?

4. Anger (questioning)
Why fuel anger's fire?

5. Anger (turning)
If the wall is too high then use low
as your new best friend. Lowness:
a new model for highness.

How difficult do you need to make it?

What is being asked of you?
The perfect lovers won't help you
decide. (They're too busy being
perfect—and they've got a lot more
perfect still to do.)

6. Anger (dissolving)
Not wrong but not quite
right. Each of you can love bigger
without guarantee of getting
bigger back.

7. Anger (replaced)
And maybe this is how you know love:
you just	know. Maddening
as that may be. Love doesn't know
the rain that opens the umbrella
invites the wind in and catches it.

Next thing you know
both of you are flying high
over bridges under covers
without worrying about holding
on. And that's how you know.
Because love told you	so.

Erotic Fiction

Oooh love to love you baby.
    —Donna Summer

1. Your first attempt at writing (erotic) fiction

You must know that he has fallen for her
quiet talk of story? Of stories written
and unwritten. A narrative bound for the literature
section certainly. But didn't you see this coming?

It happened mid-chapter. You were trying
to put it all down in words the way
you have always done and though you want
the words to stay on the page—neat and tidy—they
refuse your writerly will. Your protagonist has not
read the script you so carefully prepared. He seems
to have fallen for her words and More. He *really* wants to
read her Every Word. The ones she is writing

right now. He wants to read them. And he will.
Read them. Because he is pale from the sun
and in need of fortification. You've kept both of them
in the dark for too long and that won't do.

2. Before too long

Can a story write itself? Yes, as is most often
the case in fiction but before too long
words come unglued. Leave the page
wanting for nothing but the writing.
Any previous experience you might have
picked up in undergrad workshops seems
entirely lacking. Maybe a glimpse of pale
English skin. A slender wrist naked and
exposed. Rain on the windows.

Lots of white space left for the imagination
to wander. For the reader to wonder.
The steamiest of scenes best left to write
themselves later. The book fallen off
the bed. The sheets twisted. The lamp
extinguished so that everything can be seen.

But one can easily see that he is wanting nothing
but her now and you become uncertain of the space
between. Uneasy complications with regard to formatting.
Rhetorical questions surrounding desire and dialogue.
Whose point of view? Certainly wanting only to write
in between the lines of what the characters don't say.

3. The plot thickens (Whose point of view?)

You may have wanted the story to remain
timeless and just out of focus but this scene
is all too clear even to you: it's a hot summer
day on a picturesque lake hidden somewhere
on a treasure map of the Canadian Shield.

In the lake.

Treading, he saw her. Saw her body
treading water. Limbs that somehow knew
what the water wanted at that time: not
much, really. And just the fact

that he could look
at her and her body
above the surface.
And also below. Also
below. Beautiful
embarrassed omniscience.

Drawn to the hungry center
of things. Not just pretending
to be needy. A longing that hurts.
Not the commitment but the connection.

In love with her thighs: yes,
certainly and her
breasts, too. A nipple
witnessed once as she came
through the glass doors
into full view. A nipple

made visible through sheer
fabric. Just for an instant. He was holding
his guitar close like a crutch. Like a
lover when she came through
the glass doors.

Just to want it in his mouth.
Yes, that is the desire that lives
between his imaginings and her delicate
parts above and below the surface.

Above and below
the surface.

No hope now of avoiding the obvious.
Your faithful readers waiting mid-summer.
Call them crazy as witnesses to her treading.

Her curves curving.
Holding the water unafraid. Beyond
wetness where water has its sway.
Sunlit and dark. The space in
between.

4. Embarrassed omniscience

She couldn't see him. All the better
for her not seeing him which turned
into him seeing her more. Naked and skin
deep. He saw her. Felt her seeing
him too maybe unless he was just seeing from below
the waistline of the forest's edge where it
meets the water. Maybe he was just being
a boy. A man. A boy letting his high school
thoughts run away to that place

where the imagination makes skin-on-skin
possible. Seeing her more now.

Enough to frame the erotics of poetry and
fiction that shy away from the image
he has of her writing herself naked.

Her breasts, freckled he thinks.
Kissing them: he was
wanting to. Gently steering
the ties of her dress
away from her body's need
to be tied.

Freeing her breasts so that kissing them was
entirely inconceivably irrevocably and possibly
the most important freeing he has been part of
in a long long while.

5. Oh so soft

Kissing them. Kissing her. Kissing her through
her dress. On his knees now. Behind

her. Kissing her through her dress.
Her curves curving him nicely.
His hands working and playing their way up
and down and round and
round. In and out, even. Some serious
sliding of limbs: the curve. the flat.

Finding the possibility of her:
his fingers his tongue only
as she would wish them. Want them.

Fantasy? You bet.
Active is our imagination.
Her name is not Emily nor
Amelia. Nothing
puritan like Lavinia or Clara
Victoria Evelyn Violet Milicent Florence
Emma Margaret Lily   Elizabeth.

Timing is everything he might think
to himself and trust in the gods
of timing. Just the music and the words that
slide backandforth between
them. And why not?

6. Unreliable narrator

Afternoon sun angles and
the day heating up. Did you forget
to mention he's a little
high? The water, the clouds
the sky. Stoned for
her. The waves coming
through.

Do you feel this too?
The high vault of summer sky?

You are no longer the eagle's eye.
Attempting to address the question why.
The readers turning the page already
know somehow.

Waltzing with the sky.
High lazy cirrus rhythms.
In hopes that he can openly
confess. On his knees
longing to take off
her dress.

Within the 'we' that's in your 'I'
What when where how why?

Laugh if you want harlequin skeptics but the heart might open up, soul-deep and surfacing, when the timing is right.

Wait for this:

He'll take off his clothes for her, too. Slow. Fast. Slow. Present himself to her. Strut shyly. Coy with the stupid confidence that comes from telling lust's story.

Above and below the surface
we see you now
surfacing with the questions
to all our answers. This makes it

easier to match up the prizes with the entry ballots
and we've closed our eyes. Book-marked
the spot.

7. Even softer

But it doesn't stop here. It doesn't
matter that it's a Canada Council Grant
funding our collective imagination.

And there he is

picturing her lifting up her dress
happily. So he can find the most tender
spots that need addressing.

Something more than a kiss that finds her.
A meeting. An understanding.
Her need recognized and cared for. And
knowing the feel of his lips on her lips:

above and below the surface. We're ready
for her reluctance. For her fierce rebuttal.
(Her admitting she'd rather he kissed her butt.)

Her butt. Yes. Happily, he would
with whatever layers present
themselves. That's why

he was on his knees.
behind her. (Remember?)

His tongue. The material. Pressing harder
to see if his mouth might get through
to her. Her lips. We've all been waiting
for this here in cottage country soaking in gin
and tonic. A hand down our own pants.

Turns out he has nothing but loving wishes
for her. No ill will. Just delicate intimate pleasures
shared without coital requirements. (Not at first, anyway.)
No commitment longer than turning her on.
Just turning her on. That's his way
to get off: turning her off   on.
Willing and able.

8. Whose point of view?

Is that enough for now?
It's certainly hard to leave
knowing what everyone
knows. And it's so easy

to keep going on and
on about what things
he might dare do for her.

But it's a short story on a long
hot day. Everyone knows that
Florence Emma and Violet will

return on the next rainy day
to gather up loose plot lines
and make sure that any and all
traces of forbidden feelings
for Edward Horace and Charles
are put in their proper place.

A small fire will be burning for comfort only
in mid-July's woodstove. The children playing
Risk waiting for the sun to return tomorrow.

Meantime you'll change gears. Work
on a back-burner'd poetry manuscript. Maybe
read some back-dated Cottage Life.
Have a G & T yourself. Wait and see
how the wind blows.

The lazy boat moving over
the weightless surface.

Half-full for Sure

(Genius Doesn't Happen on Decaf)

Hello: isn't that joy
balanced there on the edge
of your coffee

cup? Sing the blues
in tones beautiful and big
and full. Banish any and all thoughts
of shame and misfortune.

Half-full for sure. Your
cup deep enough to dive
down. Touch bottom
and come back up with
the dark polished bright

enough to give away
for free. Hold it up to
the light and you will see
music pour itself out
over morning.

One finger to test
the wind and the coast
sliding by close enough for love
to be seen with the naked

eye. Tell everyone you
can: drink from this cup.

And if just a glimpse of Gaspé
fully drunk on beauty is a place you've
never been: go there now.

Espresso is a page-turner
walking history forward.
Glacier deep. The light
so forgiving now that
thoughts pass through.

Lost words return
themselves to their rightful
places then scatter for beauty.

So far beyond metaphor that language
need not apply. Everything
is being given away. Some say

paint will do the trick on a day
like today with the waves
in groups of seven. Others
insist on writing the light

just so. The canvas colourful
enough to sail where
ever.

An ancient lighthouse so
there must be jagged rocks
and safe harbour. Go there
now. Half-full for sure.
Isn't that joy
there?

A Font for All Occasions

Here is some Giant Garamond
Coming your way to cheer you

up and over the wall of fonts that
have spelled your fate for so long.

Sorry to hear your news. 10-point font is
sometimes too small for Big Love. And

you *are* loved. We will continue to love
you through this routine sadness.

Prose can weigh too heavy sometimes.
Some want it spelled out in more certain

terms but there will always be poems
of course. Now, Garamond may or may not

carry more joy than Palatino. But
Arial Narrow? Courier? Lucida Console.

Tahoma. Times New Roman.
Modern No. 20. Bookman Old Style.

Baskerville. Bank Gothic. Optima. Papyrus.
Perpetua. Rockwell Extra Bold. Sathu.

And size sometimes does
and sometimes does not   matter.

American Typewriter is a font you
were always fond of. Remember how you

loved hearing the sounds of the carriage
return lining up your worlds? A simple

tab enough to put space between you
and the things you had to leave behind.

Manual labour—Underwood or Olivetti style
was often enough to exercise the demons that enjoyed it

best when you did not write. Strike the keys and
it's a different story: blistering editorials. A delicious

post script. Concise observations. Insightful conclusions.
A poem for your daughter. Just enough ink left in the ribbon

for a love note (or two). Some say love is never having
to say you're sorry for using a bigger font. And coffee

will forever remain unapologetic for how fast it
makes you type. And just between the two of us and

the love that survives spell check there likely is no
one font for all occasions. You are simply you

in all your you-ness. Breathing all that you are.
And this will always call for the writing of more poems.

Resilience
—For Heids

You fly to Cuba because swimming
up to a bar shares a certain twisted sense
of Canadian-ness. Something akin to
skating across water to go to
work. Either way ice figures
into the equation.

And your girls are so beautiful now.
Your boys growing up and into
the world in their own ways.

Not on their own time mind
you but since they are already of the mind
that there's so much time
to waste it becomes precious anyway.
Somehow it's all good.

Your calendar is unquestionably full. You
remember to order flowers, pick up
up the drywall tape, write a note
to your daughter's teacher
explaining that the assigned questions
from the Geometry Unit were torn and
missing from her text (the remaining hole
suspiciously rhomboid-like.)
Improbable lists line your day.

Don't forget to tell them about poetry.
Your neighbours who just completed the renovation
to their family room so that they could build a bigger
wall for their television screen. Do you still bother
explaining to your Mother? Questioning yet defending
your need you to write it all down.
And your Father-in-law. Tell him about Al Purdy.

He could probably relate to the high
balls and to poems written in bars.
Tell him what Al told you:
that your job is to be the *designated
oddball to your neighbours.*

Courage. Resilience. Vacuuming.
All on a regular unbalanced diet of
humility and need. You don't have to
try to stop words from saying exactly what you
want them to say. They're yours but not
yours to keep close watch over.

Maybe talk about the ways
you worry too much. Then
brag about the fabulous by-products
of your angst: ideas for writing.

Then skate up to the bar
in your swimsuit where you can drop
your list off and pay someone
else to worry about it.

No One But the Moon

No one but the moon is singing
this song. Full of itself yet thoughtful
during this delicate phase of the song

cycle. Waxing eloquent introspective.
A midnight chorus sung through bare
branches. Your window a transistor radio

pulling in the signal. Gentle traffic
hum doing nothing to interfere with
the feeling. An exquisite loneliness

to feeling this small. So familiar.
So unlike anything you've ever
heard before. A poem

whispered melody. The stars
a wash of blue light. Clouds
recognizing themselves in the opening

verse. An entire town asleep
under the influence. So much more
than verse verse chorus verse

bridge and no one
but the moon is singing
this song.

Field Notes for Jabez

I saw a beggar leaning on his wooden crutch.
He called out to me, "Don't ask for so much."

I saw a young girl leaning on her darkened door
She cried out to me, "Why not ask for more?"

Leonard Cohen felt the groove and made it
groovier by spelling it backwards: Dog.
Looking for any old fire
hydrant to do His Work. Finding

joy and fulfillment and deep pleasure in
barking up the wrong tree. So much
so that it was Right   (On). Hallelujah.
I'm your man.

Oh, that You would bless us, indeed

Tastes great *and* less filling. Not only hot
but cool. Cachet to spare.

A spiritual groove with words
and music to fuel the fire. (And sometimes
only words to measure the beat.) And words
were enough. Are enough. Will always be

enough for each and every one of us
to put our faith in. To declare our Faith.

To prepare to accept our responsibilities. More and
more each moment. To prepare to do Good
Work. Why not engage with the world in all the ways
that enable us to give our Gifts ?

And enlarge our territory.

We can't do this on our own and so we ask
for Help in moving into the beautiful
unknown of Your Work.

Key turning points that we are beginning
to feel rather than think   through.
A visceral sense of good   timing.
Homework paying   off.
.

A quiet wish to move within the Spirit
that moves. To do what we could not
do without You. Praying for signs and
possibilities through difficult days.

Embarrassed to be invoking God
as an opportunist only. To be in dialogue
with God from the perspective of one who
wants and needs. Always a little confusion
on how to be of Service. Particularly

during those times when our song
feels so small and weak. (Like a bird
on a wire.) Still so much
room for work and play and abundance.

Our way is our way but really
Thy Way despite our hesitancy
to use upper case on Spiritual Matters.

We work on the Love Project because
we have to. Because it's all we can do on
Monday morning when the water is not
so warm that swimming is the first thing
we want to do. The River not the first place
we might choose to make a big splash.

Doubt. Delay. Over-thinking. More Thoughts.
Uncertainty. Love. Grace. Gifts. Abundance.
Insight. Imagination. Forgiveness. Clarity. Love.

That Your Hand would be with us.

Not so serious ok? God's smile and a good laugh.
Bend and sway. Never break. Some of us are
simply looking for Love. Looking to Believe.
Invoking Faith. Asking for direction. Willing.

Small steps: ok. Baby Steps: good.
Big steps fine, too. But one step
at a time. One step at a time.

Show us a sign gear Dog—dear God.
Hear our dyslexic prayer. Show us
a sign. Let us listen. Take notice.

No Matter What   as a mantra.
Stretching for acceptance and understanding.
Asking forgiveness for blindness and other
assorted shortcomings.

That You would keep us from evil.

Bless us Big time is all we're asking.
In this moment heaven sends angels
mortgage payments, missing socks
strength, useful one-liners, tiny love
notes folded neatly with the laundry
along with people we might need and
people who might need   us.

And if nothing else:
That we not cause pain.

Great Big Love

Does anyone here feel it might be entirely possible
to have never truly experienced Love?

To have never loved? To have never
been loved? Truly? (And it is a Great Big Love

being spoken of here.) The Giving. The
Receiving. (Pause here to let silence settle

into itself.) I wonder about these things myself
and I'm wondering if you wonder too?

Have you ever really loved? Really
been loved? What if noisy response and

humorous anecdotes were not permitted?
What if embarrassment and shame were not options?

What if the body's automatic response designed
to ensure that such knowledge never makes

its way to the light of day was circumvented? What if
you just let yourself be here? Now. Drop down deep

enough to touch bottom and rise to the surface
where the dark is accompanied by light.

A mansion in the slums. A suburban castle.
A shack high in the hills above it all.

A home where you know with certainty you belong.
A window on the world—grand and forgiving.

You can see Everything. Mountains forming.
Weather being made and unmade. Humanity

stumbling toward failure and redemption.
The Window is wide open. The Window is door-like

in its ability to open out on the world.
One can only feel safe here on either side

knowing that risk is the only way to feel.
The only way to see. Towering forests live here.

Sweeping grasslands. Brilliant lakes.
Barren plains. Marsh. Muskeg. Bogs.

Flowing gardens. Rich black soil.
Cracked earth and concrete. Glass

towers. Sprawling industrial parks. Lost
canyons. Dizzying cliffs. The only way to

risk knowing how to feel. Dark and
light and Everything. Silence. Love.

Does anyone here feel it might be
entirely possible?

Another Poem for You

Yes. I will say it
in the first line: this poem
is for you. All of you.

Every part that I am learning
by heart to love. By hearts. Yours
and mine. This is my job so why not
make it a poem about love? The coin

is shiny and paper is as good
as gold and we don't yet know how
it all comes out in the wash. But again

it's my job to at least report on love
by way of cinquain, diamante, free
verse, glosa, ghazal. (Strangely, if you take
the time to mispronounce or misspell
the latter—why is it that the gazelle

is the one chosen always to be outrun
by the liontigercheetah and we compelled to watch
as a substantial hunk of its flesh is torn off in front
of the camera). Maybe that's the way it goes
in grassy plain'd haikus but that's not love.

Nor does love necessarily move up
or down the food chain. Poems in the shape
of a heart? More or less like   love I suppose.

Still I can't be sure. And why these
digressions? When I could just come out
and pronounce it right off the hop. This is
a love poem. For you. For every part of you.

If I happen to pounce it would only be
to surprise you with love's greeting: a gentle
nip, a nibble perhaps in the interest of
sinking my teeth into a much bigger love story.

Sometime later   watching
The Wild Kingdom documentary run
backwards—the gazelle of course chases
the liontigercheetah awkwardly at high speed
ass-first putting a fresh spin on chance
encounters in beautiful exotic settings.

As a form, the ghazal is shot to hell
but love is flesh and blood and always willing
to bleed in ways that poets find hard
to resist and perhaps this is all
that need be said. I will take the time—
admit in front of the camera: I've never written
a ghazal but love is my job so why not
make it a poem for   you?

End Notes

Writing Songs
The opening and closing italicized stanzas are taken from "Another Year of Song" composed by GW Rasberry, J. Campbell & R. Unger (Fireweed) from GW Rasberry's (2006) album, *Curving for the Coast*.

Wisdom Come
The line "And when will the days of wisdom come?" is taken from Annie Dillard's (2007) novel, *The Maytrees*.

Field Notes for Jabez
This poem is based on a close reading of Bruce Wilkinson's (2000) book *The Prayer of Jabez. Breaking Through to the Blessed Life*.

The opening lyrics are from Leonard Cohen's song "Like a Bird on the Wire" from his (1969) album, *Songs from a Room*.

Gary Rasberry:

Gary Rasberry. Philosopher. Poet. Imagination Consultant. Musician. Artist. Educator. Insecure Extrovert. Reluctant Enthusiast. Risk-taker. Scaredy Cat. Small Animal with Fast Metabolism.

A Connector-of-Dots, Gary brings people & ideas together. He works & plays with language: Words. Melodies. Poetry. Lyrics. Songs. Stories. Spoken Word. Aphorisms. Essays. Dissertations. 'To Do' Lists.

Gary works & plays with children. He Sings. Talks. Tells Stories. Imagines. Composes. Creates. Reads. Listens. Loves. Laughs. He also works and plays with people who are busy asking the question, "How Do We Learn to Create a Life that Matters?"

Gary Rasberry lives in Kingston, Ontario where he teaches songwriting workshops at Queen's University and offers Song, Story & Sound workshops in schools everywhere. Currently touring with The Big Idea Band, Gary is doing shows with his latest musical release, "What's the Big Idea?!?"

Books in the North Shore Series
Find full information at
– http://www.HiddenBrookPress.com/b-NShore.html

2 Anthologies

Changing Ways is a book of prose by Cobourg area authors including: Jean Edgar Benitz, Patricia Calder, Fran O'Hara Campbell, Leonard D'Agostino, Shane Joseph, Brian Mullally. Editor: Jacob Hogeterp
– Prose – ISBN – 978-1-897475-22-5

That Not Forgotten - Editor – Bruce Kauffman with 118 authors from the North Shore geographic area.
– Prose and Poetry – ISBN – 978-1-897475-89-8

First set of five books

— M.E. Csamer – Kingston – *A Month Without Snow*
– Prose – ISBN – 978-1-897475-87-2
— Elizabeth Greene – Kingston – *The Iron Shoes*
– Poetry – ISBN – 978-1-897475-76-6
— Richard Grove – Brighton – *A Family Reunion*
– Prose – ISBN – 978-1-897475-90-2
— R.D. Roy – Trenton – *A Pre emptive Kindness*
– Prose – ISBN – 978-1-897475-80-3
— Eric Winter – Cobourg – *The Man In The Hat*
– Poetry – ISBN – 978-1-897475-77-3

Second set of five books

— Janet Richards – Belleville – *Glass Skin*
– Poetry – ISBN – 978-1-897475-01-0
— R.D. Roy – Trenton – *Three Cities*
– Poetry – ISBN – 978-1-897475-96-4
— Wayne Schlepp – Cobourg – *The Darker Edges of the Sky*
– Poetry – ISBN – 978-1-897475-99-5
— Benjamin Sheedy – Kingston – *A Centre in Which They Breed*
– Poetry – ISBN – 978-1-897475-98-8
— Patricia Stone – Peterborough – *All Things Considered*
– Prose – ISBN – 978-1-897475-04-1
– Prose – ISBN – 978-1-897475-37-9

Third set of five books

— Mark Clement – Cobourg – *Island In the Shadow*
  – Poetry – ISBN – 978-1-897475-08-9
— Anthony Donnelly – Brighton – *Fishbowl Fridays*
  – Prose – ISBN – 978-1-897475-02-7
— Chris Faiers – Marmora – *ZenRiver Poems & Haibun*
  – Poetry – ISBN – 978-1-897475-25-6
— Shane Joseph – Cobourg – *Fringe Dwellers* Second Edition
  – Prose – ISBN – 978-1-897475-44-7
— Deborah Panko – Cobourg – *Somewhat Elsewhere*
  – Poetry – ISBN – 978-1-897475-13-3

Forth set of five books

— Diane Dawber – Bath – *Driving, Braking and Getting out to Walk*
  – Poetry – ISBN – 978-1-897475-40-9
— Patrick Gray – Port Hope – *This Grace of Light*
  – Poetry – ISBN – 978-1-897475-34-8
— John Pigeau – Kingston – *The Nothing Waltz*
  – Prose – ISBN – 978-1-897475-37-9
— Mike Johnston – Cobourg – *Reflections Around the Sun*
  – Poetry – ISBN – 978-1-897475-38-6
— Kathryn MacDonald – Shannonville – *Calla & Édourd*
  – Prose – ISBN – 978-1-897475-39-3

Fifth set of three books

— Tara Kainer – Kingston – *When I Think On Your Lives*
  – Poetry– ISBN – 978-1-897475-68-3
— Morgan Wade – Kingston – *The Last Stoic*
  – Novel – ISBN – 978-1-897475-63-8
— Kathryn MacDonald – Shannonville – *A Breeze You Whisper*
  – Poetry – ISBN – 978-1-897475-66-9

Sixth set of three books

— Bruce Kauffman – Kingston – *The Texture of Days, in Ash and Leaf*
  – Poetry – ISBN - 978-1-897475-86-7
— Chris Faiers – Marmora – *Eel Pie Island Dharma: A hippie memoir/haibun*
  – A memoir in haibun form – ISBN - 978-1-897475-92-8
— Theodore Michael Christou – Kingston – *an overbearing eye*
  – Poety – ISBN – 978-1-897475-93-5

Seventh set of four books

— Alyssa Cooper – Kingston – *Cold Breath of Life*
  – Poetry – ISBN – 978-1-927725-02-3
— Bruce Kauffman – Kingston – *The Silence Before the Whisper Comes*
  – Poetry – ISBN – 978-1-897475-98-0
— Sarah Richardson – Kingston – *Before I Lose Light*
  – Poetry – ISBN – 978-1-927725-05-4
— G. W. Rasberry – Kingston – *More Naked Than Ever*
  – Poetry – ISBN – 978-1-927725-04-7

www.ingramcontent.com/pod-product-compliance
Lightning Source LLC
Chambersburg PA
CBHW060504080526
44584CB00015B/1546